ALL MEN ARE PIGS!

ALL MEN ARE PIGS!

Compiled by
DAVID AND JACKUM BROWN

MICHAEL O'MARA BOOKS LIMITED

First published in Great Britain in 1999 by
Michael O'Mara Books Limited
9 Lion Yard
Tremadoc Road
London SW4 7NQ

A CIP catalogue record for this book is available from
the British Library

ISBN 1-85479-452-3

1 3 5 7 9 10 8 6 4 2

Designed and typeset by Keystroke, Jacaranda Lodge, Wolverhampton

Printed and bound by Cox & Wyman, Reading

CONTENTS

With thanks to

Sarah Copeland,
Jon Goddard,
Fraser Harrison
and
Jean-François Raymond

Introduction:
Give a Hog a Bad Name

Your average friendly Martian, landing on earth for the first time, would probably be pretty astonished by just about everything. One of the strangest things for It (we shall assume that Martians are not troubled by gender) to observe would be the habits of the six billion two-footed creatures that would seem to be all over the place.

It would notice that while these humans came in a rather limited range of colours, and were available in a restricted variety of sizes, from very small to not very big, there did seem to be two distinct types of the species.

The first type, the more shapely and often better-smelling of the two, would be observed looking after the small ones, washing, cleaning, ironing, tidying things up, and frequently growing all the food and fetching all the water too.

The second type, the bemused Martian would notice, was a bit bigger and taller but usually with less hair. They could be seen meeting, talking and drinking a lot, often while watching others of their kind throwing, kicking, and hitting balls of various sizes.

On closer inspection of human habits, the Martian would become even more puzzled. It would learn that, among other things, men made jokes about their wives' mothers, went bald, governed most countries of the world, and were very keen on cars; It would also discover that women were capable of multiple orgasms, lived longer, got paid less for more work, and spent a lot of time and money on clothes and make-up in order to attract men. Oh, and that only they gave birth.

You can't help feeling more than a bit of sympathy for the Martian's puzzlement. It does seem odd, too, that most of the disagreeable manifestations of human behaviour are committed by men. Men are much more likely to vandalize, to rob or to murder – indeed, to commit every crime (except prostitution) – than women. Men are responsible for virtually all sex crimes; when did you last read about a man being gang-raped by a group of violent young women?

Ever since Adam met Eve, men have spent a lot of their energies in lording it over women, treating them like slaves or sex objects while themselves generally strutting their stuff. Happily – if that's the word – all this piggishness has been well documented. It seems that almost as soon as men could write anything down at all they started writing male-chauvinistic things about women. The worlds of ancient Greece and Rome were obviously filled with men being piggish and expressing male-chauvinistic views. Homer, Ovid, Cato the Elder, Juvenal and Cicero – they were all piggish, if their writings are anything to go by. The Bible, particularly the Old Testament, is a pretty rich source of male chauvinism, too.

For many centuries women clearly endured men's piggish – sometimes downright swinish – behaviour with forbearance. They were probably wise to keep their complaints to themselves. The mildest resistance to male piggery, expressed in public, would have brought men's aggressive violence down upon their heads with even greater fury than usual. They probably would have been – and indeed many were, at one stage in history – burned at the stake.

It's worth remembering that women in Britain and America only won the right to vote less than a hundred years ago. Since then they have made great progress towards equality with men, but male attitudes are like an iceberg – a visible mass with a far greater bulk, the real danger, lurking beneath the surface. As you will see from this book, women have been trying to make up for lost time and, particularly in the last thirty years, have become vehemently vocal on the subject of male piggishness.

We are often hearing that young men are increasingly confused as to what their role as males should be

– and recent advances in genetic engineering must give them anxiety attacks. Now, even years after a man's death, his partner can decide to conceive and give birth using his own carefully stored sperm. Even more scary – for men anyway – the Massachusetts Institute of Technology is currently working to produce a viable embryo from the DNA of two *female* mice. It may be, therefore, that men are soon going to be as much use as manual typewriters.

While this may be the best thing for the species in the end – or at least for women – pity the poor old pig for a moment. Aside from being a rather messy eater, the pig appears to share very few of the male human being's more unpleasant characteristics. Do pigs beat their wives? Do pigs go to war? Do pigs get road rage? Do pigs throw their dirty pants on the bedroom floor and expect them to be picked up and washed?

If pigs were ever to be asked their opinion, one may assume they'd be pretty miffed at this taking of their name in vain. In fact, they'd probably go the whole hog and eat all men. It would be very messy.

So, gentle reader, if you're one of those people who thinks that men have been having a bit of a rough time of it recently, read on . . . and think again.

1 SWINESPEAK

men being pompous, pretentious, dismissive
of women; men and art and culture

So go to your quarters now and attend to your own work, the loom and the spindle, and tell the servants to get on with theirs. Talking must be the men's concern, and mine in particular; for I am master in this house.

Homer (ninth century BC), Ionian poet, from the Odyssey, Book I

And you would not be wide of the mark if you thought that I would insist that women should know how to dance: call for the wine and let her move her arms when she is told.

Ovid (43 BC–?AD 17), Roman poet, from The Art of Love

Among them was Sempronia, a woman guilty of many misdeeds which showed she was as bold and reckless as a man ... she knew a lot about Greek and Latin literature and more about lyre playing and dancing than was proper for a respectable woman, not to mention many other talents of a degenerate nature. Modesty and chastity were low on her list of priorities ... she was of such a passionate nature that she made advances to men more often than they did to her.

Sallust (86–34 BC), Roman historian, from Catilina

It is not accidental that when God became 'man' He chose to be a male. There's no doubt that He could have chosen to be a woman if He'd wanted to.

The Rt Rev. and Rt Hon. Graham Leonard, Bishop of London, British churchman and writer on religious and theological matters, arguing against women priests in the Church of England; Sunday Times, *22 December 1985*

The Blessed One said, 'Amrapali, the mind of a woman is easily disturbed and misled. She yields to her desires and surrenders to jealousy more easily than a man. Therefore it is more difficult for a woman to follow the Noble Path.'

The Teachings of Buddha, fifth century BC

Women want total freedom, or rather total licence. If you allow them to achieve complete equality with men, do you think they will be any easier to live with? Not at all. Once they have achieved equality, they will be your masters.

Cato the Elder (234–149 BC), Roman statesman and writer

The beauty of a woman is only skin deep. If men could only see what is beneath the flesh and penetrate below the surface with eyes like the Boeotian lynx, they would be nauseated just to look at women, for all this feminine charm is nothing but phlegm, blood, humours, gall.

Odo of Cluny (879–942), French abbot and saint

No vote can be given by lunatics, idiots, minors, aliens, females, persons convicted of perjury, subornation of perjury, bribery treating or undue influence, or by those tainted of felony or outlawed in a criminal suit.

Sir William Blackstone (1723–80), British jurist, from Commentaries on the Laws of England

You will find that the woman who is really kind to dogs is always one who has failed to inspire sympathy in men.

Max Beerbohm (1872–1956), British writer, critic and wit, from Zuleika Dobson

For the lips of a strange woman drop as an honeycomb, and her mouth is smoother than oil: but her end is bitter as wormwood, sharp as a two-edged sword.

Old Testament: Proverbs 5: 3–4

Certain women should be struck regularly, like gongs.

Noël Coward (1899–1973), British dramatist, actor and composer, from Private Lives

And a woman is only a woman, but a good cigar is a smoke.

Rudyard Kipling (1865–1936), British poet, short-story writer and novelist, from 'The Betrothed'

The First Blast of the Trumpet Against the Monstrous Regiment of Women.

John Knox (1514–72), Scottish religious reformer, pamphlet title, 1558

The Professor of Gynaecology began his course of lectures as follows: Gentlemen, woman is an animal that micturates once a day, defecates once a week, menstruates once a month, parturates once a year and copulates whenever she has the opportunity.

W. Somerset Maugham (1874–1965), British writer, from A Writer's Notebook

When a woman becomes a scholar there is usually something wrong with her sexual organs.

Friedrich Wilhelm Nietzsche (1844–1900), German philosopher, poet and critic

In her particular nature, woman is defective and misbegotten . . . the production of woman is due to a weakness in the generative force or imperfection in the pre-existing matter or even from some external influences, for example the humid winds from the south.

St Thomas Aquinas (1225–74), Italian theologian, philosopher and Dominican friar

The meaning of woman is to be meaningless. She represents negation, the opposite pole from the Godhead, the other possibility of humanity.

Otto Weininger (1880–1903), Austrian philosopher of influence in the Nazi movement, notably for his anti-semitism

Men should be trained for war and women for the recreation of the warrior; all else is folly.

Friedrich Wilhelm Nietzsche (1844–1900), German philosopher, poet and critic

A woman's place is in the home looking after the family, not out working.

Pope John Paul II, 1981

If all women were enfranchised they would at once swamp the votes of men.

Samuel Evans (1859–1918), MP for Glamorgan, British judge and politician, House of Commons, 1906

Nothing would induce me to vote for giving women the franchise. I am not going to be hen-pecked into a question of such importance.

Winston Churchill (1874–1965), British statesman, orator and writer, c.1910

 SAYINGS AND PROVERBS

Maidens should be seen and not heard.

A sieve will hold water better than a woman's mouth a secret.

When an ass climbs a ladder we may find wisdom in women.

A woman, a dog and a walnut tree,
The harder you beat them the better they'll be.

A woman's place is in the home.

A woman's work is never done.

A woman has the form of an angel, the heart of a serpent, and the mind of an ass.

German

Women have long hair and short brains.

Women and sparrows twitter in company.

Japanese

Women are necessary evils.

Women are the devil's nets.

Women are the snares of Satan.

Women in state affairs are like monkeys in glass shops.

There are many females who never feel any sexual
excitement whatever. The best mothers, wives, and
managers of households, know little or nothing of sexual
indulgences. Love of home, children, and domestic duties
are the only passions they feel.

W. Acton, from The Functions and Disorders of the Reproductive Organs,
1865

What women want is not to be treated with respect and
care. They want to be treated like shit. They seem to like it.

John Steed, British rapist and murderer, referring to his crime of 1986

Therefore women should not be pushed forward or
allowed to have prominence in those spheres where
Allah has assigned them an inferior position. This is vital
for decency and for maintaining equilibrium in the Society;
otherwise there will be moral chaos, social imbalance and
corruption as is being witnessed today because of the
prominence of women in economic, political and social
pursuits.

Muhammad Imram, from Ideal Women in Islam, *1979*

But nothing could easily be found that is more remark-able than the monthly flux of women. Contact with it turns new wine sour, crops touched by it become barren, grafts die, seeds in gardens are dried up, the fruit of trees falls off, the bright surface of mirrors in which it is merely reflected is dimmed, the edge of steel and the gleam of ivory are dulled, hives of bees die, even bronze and iron are at once seized by rust, and a horrible smell fills the air; to taste it drives dogs mad and infects their bites with an incurable poison.

Pliny the Elder (AD 23–79), Roman writer and scholar

A man without a woman is like a neck without a pain.

W. C. Fields (1880–1946), US film actor

Women must come off the pedestal. Men put us up there to get us out of the way.

Viscountess Rhondda, British aristocrat

John, after his beating me at chess had had the satisfaction of teaching me. If he wallops me absolutely he remarks 'A good game. You're getting on.' If it is a draw he exclaims 'My God I'm a complete idiot. I've lost my head completely.' This strikes me as very male.

Katherine Mansfield (1888–1923), New Zealand-born British short-story writer, of her husband, the British writer and critic John Middleton Murry (1889–1957)

Male culture seems to have abandoned the breadwinner role without overcoming the sexist attitudes that role has perpetuated: on the one hand, the expectations of female nurturance and submissive service as a matter of right; on the other hand, a misogynist contempt for women as 'parasites' and entrappers of men.

Barbara Ehrenreich and Deirdre English, US feminist writers

To tell a woman using her mind that she is thinking with a man's brain means telling her that she can't think with her own brain; it demonstrates your [men's] ineradicable belief in her intellectual inadequacy.

Françoise Parturier, French writer

A man at his desk in a room with a closed door is a man at work. A woman at a desk in any room is available.

Betty Rollin, US writer

Ritual verbal gang-banging is so staple an ingredient of ordinary respectable man-to-man conversation that any objection to it is taken as a tasteless assault on an inoffensive form of pleasantry.

Dorothy Dinerstein, US feminist

A man is entitled to issue blunt orders, contradict people flatly, instruct or command or forbid outright, without apology or circumlocution.

Ibid.

I discovered that even now men prefer women to be less informed, less able, less talkative, and certainly less self-centred than they are themselves; so I generally obliged them.

Jan Morris, British writer, formerly a man

There are no father-in-law jokes.

Bernice Sandler, US psychologist

Men trivialize the talk of women not because they are afraid of any such talk, but in order to make women themselves downgrade it.

Carolyn Heilbrun, US educationalist

The male brain, now, that's a different matter. Only a thin connection. Space over here, time over there, music and arithmetic in their own sealed compartments. The right brain doesn't know what the left is doing. Good for aiming, though, for hitting the target when you pull the trigger. What's the target? Who cares? What matters is hitting it. That's the male brain for you. Objective.

Margaret Atwood, Canadian poet and novelist

To envision a Chinese nobleman's wife or courtesan with daintily slippered three-inch stubs in place of normal feet is to understand much about men's violent subjugation of women.

Susan Brownmiller, US writer

Through all the ages of the world's history the more power-ful sex has been liable to use their power carelessly, not for protection only, but for pain.

Josephine Butler (1828–1906), English feminist writer

Just as footbinding was required by the men of China, so is mindbinding a universal demand of patriarchal males.

Mary Daly, US feminist philosopher

The value of the penis lies mainly not in its charm as a water toy, or in its magic erectile properties, but rather in the social prerogatives it confers.

Dorothy Dinerstein, US feminist

Police and court data indicate that women are much more likely to be seriously assaulted or murdered by men known to them.

R. E. Dobash and R. Dobash, British writers

Male dominance is the environment we know, in which we must live.

Andrea Dworkin, US feminist

Men define intelligence, men define usefulness, men tell us what is beautiful, men even tell us what is womanly.

Sally Kempton, US writer

Vain creature, you do not want a woman who knows how to forgive, you want a woman who pretends to believe you have never done anything that needs forgiveness. You want her to caress the hand that strikes her and kiss the mouth that lies to her.

George Sand (Amandine Lucie Aurore Dupin, Baronne Dudevant; 1804–76),
French novelist and champion of women's rights to independence

In a patriarchy, a poor man's house may be his castle, but even a rich woman's body is not her own.

Gloria Steinem, US feminist

When a man gets up to speak, people listen then look. When a woman gets up, people look; then, if they like what they see, they listen.

Pauline Frederick (1883–1938), US actress

When men are oppressed, it's tragedy. When women are oppressed, it's tradition.

Bernadette Mosala, South African feminist

Women age, but men mature.

Gloria Steinem, US feminist

The reason most men feel comfortable making jokes directed at women is that they do not expect any viable retort.

Regina Barreca, US humorist

So, if woman received her crookedness from the rib, and consequently from the Man, how doth man excell in crookedness, who has more of those crooked ribs?

'Esther Sowerman', early seventeenth-century English writer, from Esther Hath Hang'd Haman, *1619, a reply to* The Arraignment of Lewd, Idle, Forward and Unconstant Woman, *by Joseph Swetnam*

When a man can't explain a woman's actions, the first thing he thinks about is the condition of her uterus.

Clare Boothe Luce (1903–87), US writer, playwright, journalist, politician and diplomat

Men say they love independence in a woman, but they don't waste a second demolishing it brick by brick.

Candice Bergen, US film actress

When a man gives his opinion he's a man. When a woman gives her opinion she's a bitch.

Bette Davis (1908–89), US film actress

Women speak because they wish to speak, whereas a man speaks only when driven to speech by something outside himself — like, for instance, he can't find any clean socks.

Jean Kerr, US playwright

When a woman looks at a man in evening dress, she sometimes can't help wondering why he wants to blazon his ancestry to the world by wearing a coat with a long tail to it.

Helen Rowland (1875–1950), US writer and journalist

The lust of domination was probably the first effect of the Fall; and as there was no other intelligent being over whom to exercise it, woman was the first victim of this unhallowed passion . . . All history attests that man has subjected woman to his will, used her as a means to promote his selfish gratification, to minister to his sensual pleasures, to be instrumental in promoting his comfort; but never has he desired to elevate her to that rank she was created to fill. He has done all he could to debase and enslave her mind; and now he looks triumphantly on the ruin he has wrought, and says, the being he has thus deeply injured is his inferior.

Sarah Moore Grimke (1792–1873), US reformer, from Letters on the Equality of the Sexes

Poor Mary Ann! She gave the guy an inch and now he thinks he's a ruler.

Mae West (1893–1980), US film actress

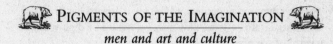

PIGMENTS OF THE IMAGINATION
men and art and culture

Man is active, full of movement, creative in politics, business and culture. The male shapes and moulds society and the world. Woman, on the other hand, is passive. She stays at home as is her nature. She is matter waiting to be formed by the active male principle. Of course the active elements are always higher on any scale, and more divine. Man consequently plays a major part in reproduction; the woman is merely the passive incubator of his seed.

Aristotle (384–322 BC), Greek philosopher, Politics, Book I

Women ruin music. If the ladies are ill-favoured the men do not want to play next to them, and if they are well-favoured, they can't.

Sir Thomas Beecham (1879–1961), British conductor

There are no women composers, never have been, and possibly never will be.

Ibid.

Although the witch, incarnate or in surrogate-mother disguise, remains a universal bogey, pejorative aspects of the wizard, her masculine counterpart, have vanished over the patriarchal centuries. The term wizard has acquired reverential status – wizard of finance, wizard of diplomacy, wizard of science.

Dena Justin, US writer and educationalist, 'From Mother Goddess to Dishwasher', Natural History, February 1973

A female poet, a female author of any kind, ranks below an actress, I think.

Charles Lamb (1775–1834), British essayist

Literature cannot be the business of a woman's life, and it ought not to be. The more she is engaged in her proper duties, the less leisure will she have for it, even as an accomplishment and a recreation.

Robert Southey (1774–1843), British poet

I would venture that Anon., who wrote so many poems without signing them, was often a woman.

Virginia Woolf (1882–1941), British novelist and critic

The true artist will let his wife slave, his children go barefoot, his mother drudge for him at seventy, sooner than work at anything but his art.

George Bernard Shaw (1856–1950), Irish playwright, essayist and critic

Nobody objects to a woman being a good writer or sculptor or geneticist if at the same time she manages to be a good wife, good mother, good-looking, good-tempered, well groomed and unaggressive.

Leslie M. McIntyre

Men painters mostly despise women painters.

Emily Carr (1871–1945), Canadian artist

Literary men, when they like women at all, do not want literary women. What they want is girls.

Muriel Spark, British novelist

Just as more and more women were getting paid for using their brains, more and more men represented them in novels, plays and poems as nothing but bodies.

Sandra M. Gilbert and Susan Gubar, US feminists

It is no small irony that, while the very social fabric of our male-dominated culture denies women equal access to political, economic and legal power, the literature, myth and humour or our culture depict women not only as the power behind the throne, but the real source of the oppression of men.

Susan Griffin, US feminist writer

When men write about the family, they're thought to be using it as a metaphor for something larger. Women, on the other hand, are seen as writing domestic soap opera.

Sue Miller, US writer

Why is it difficult to find men who are sensitive, caring and good-looking? They all already have boyfriends.

Anon.

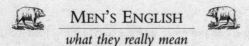

MEN'S ENGLISH
what they really mean

I'm hungry.   *I'm hungry.*

I'm sleepy.   *I'm sleepy.*

I'm tired.   *I'm tired.*

Do you want to go to   *I'd eventually like to have*
a movie?   *sex with you.*

Can I take you out to   *I'd eventually like to have*
dinner?   *sex with you.*

Can I call you sometime?	*I'd eventually like to have sex with you.*
May I have this dance?	*I'd eventually like to have sex with you.*
Nice dress!	*Nice cleavage/high hemline!*
What's wrong?	*I don't see why you are making such a big deal out of this.*
What's wrong?	*What meaningless self-inflicted psychological trauma are you going through now?*
What's wrong?	*I guess sex tonight is out of the question.*
I'm bored.	*Do you want to have sex, or something?*
I love you.	*Let's have sex now.*
I love you, too.	*Okay, I said it . . . we'd better have sex now!*

Let's talk.

I am a deep person. Maybe you'd like to have sex with me?

Will you marry me?

I want to make it a breach of contract for you to have sex with other men.

I like that one better.

Pick any damn dress and let's go home!

I don't think that blouse and that skirt go well together.

I am gay.

That's interesting, dear.

Are you still talking?

That's women's work.

It's difficult, dirty, and thankless.

I don't need to read the instructions.

I am perfectly capable of screwing it up without printed help.

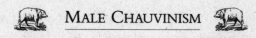

MALE CHAUVINISM

How do you know when a woman's about to say something smart?

When she starts her sentence with 'A man once told me . . .'.

How many male chauvinist pigs does it take to change a light bulb?

Oh, just let the bitch cook in the dark!

What's worse than a male chauvinist pig?

A woman who won't do as she's told.

Why do women have smaller feet than men?

So they can stand closer to the kitchen sink.

How do you fix a woman's watch?

You don't. There's a clock on the oven.

Why do women rub their eyes when they wake up in the morning?

Because they don't have balls to scratch.

If your dog is barking at the back door and your wife is yelling at the front door, which do you let in first?

The dog of course . . . at least he'll shut up after you let him in.

What do you call a woman who has lost 95 per cent of her intelligence?

Divorced.

The three fastest means of communication, according to men:

telephone
television
tell a woman

Joe said, 'Know what, Charlie? I killed five flies yesterday, three males and two females.'

'How could you tell them apart, Joe?' asked Charlie.

Joe replied, 'That was easy. The three males were sitting on a case of beer and the two females were on the phone.'

An English professor wrote the words, 'Woman without her man is nothing' on the blackboard and directed the students to punctuate it correctly.

The men wrote: 'Woman, without her man, is nothing.'

The women wrote: 'Woman! Without her, man is nothing.'

Have you ever noticed how many of women's problems can be traced to the male gender? MENstruation, MENopause, MENtal breakdown, GUYnecology, HIMmorrhoids

2 DAYS OF SWINE AND ROSES

men and marriage and courtship

Of all living, thinking beings, we women are the most unlucky. First of all we have a dowry which must buy a husband to control our bodies; not having a husband is worse. Secondly, there is the important question: is he a good or a bad husband? Women have no easy way out of marriage and cannot say no to their husbands.

Euripides (?480–406 BC), Greek tragic dramatist, from Medea

A man who finds his wife tedious can relieve the boredom by going out with a friend of his own age; but a woman must not let her eyes stray from the only man in her life.

Ibid.

Still, better to have a musical wife than a flat-chested, straight-faced woman who dashes boldly about all over town, turning up at all-male gatherings, telling generals in uniform just what to do – and while her husband is there, too.

Juvenal (AD ?60–?140), Roman satirist, from Satires

A woman without a man is like a fish without a bicycle.

Gloria Steinem, US feminist

When you see what some girls marry, you realize how they must hate to work for a living.

Helen Rowland (1876–1950), US writer and journalist

I married beneath me. All women do.

Nancy, Lady Astor (1879–1964), British politician

Bigamy is when you're married to one man too many. Monogamy is the same thing.

Erica Jong, US writer

It should be a very happy marriage – they are both so much in love with him.

Irene Thomas, British writer and broadcaster

Some of my colleagues are so keen on family values that they choose to have more than one of them.

Edwina Currie, British politician and novelist

I hope the dress brings someone more happiness than it brought me. On our wedding day, Marco said he didn't like it.

Lisa, ex-wife of chef and restaurateur Marco Pierre White, on donating her wedding dress to a charity raffle

I have been this ten days in debate whether I should hang or marry, in which time I have cried some two hours every day and knocked my head against the wall some fifteen times.

Lady Mary Wortley Montagu (1689–1782), British woman of letters, in a letter to her friend, Miss Philippa Mundy, 2 November 1711

Olinda . . . this marrying I do not like: 'tis like going on a long voyage to sea, where after a while even the calms are distasteful, and the storms are dangerous: one seldom sees a new object, 'tis still a deal of sea, sea, husband, husband, every day, – till one's quite cloyed with it.

Aphra Behn (1640–89), English dramatist and novelist, from her play The Dutch Lover

The state of matrimony is a dangerous disease: far better to take drink in my opinion.

Madame de Sevigné (Marie de Rabutin-Chantal, Marquise de Sevigné; 1626–96), French letter writer

I'd rather be flayed alive! Ugh! married to Hugh! I should be dead of disgust in a week! Faugh!

Rhoda Broughton (1840–1920), British novelist, from Cometh Up As A Flower

For a pair of first-class blue eyes warranted a fast colour, for ditto superfine red lips, for so many pounds of prime white flesh, he has paid down a handsome price on the nail, without any haggling, and now if he may not test the worth of his purchases, poor man, he is hardly used! As for me, I sit tolerable still, and am not yet actually sick.

Ibid.

I am happy now that Charles calls on my bedchamber less frequently than of old. As it is, I now endure but two calls a week and when I hear his steps outside my door I lie down on my bed, close my eyes, open my legs and think of England.

Lady Alice Hillingdon (1857–1940), English aristocrat and writer

In love, as in pain, in shock, in trouble.

Germaine Greer, Australian feminist and writer

Oh girls! set your affections on cats, poodles, parrots or lap dogs; but let matrimony alone. It's the hardest way on earth of getting a living.

Fanny Fern (Sara Payson Parton, née Willis; 1811–72), US writer

If any man take a wife, and go in unto her, and hate her, And give occasions of speech against her, and bring up an evil name upon her, and say, I took this woman, and when I came to her, I found her not a maid: Then shall the father of the damsel, and her mother, take and bring forth the tokens of the damsel's virginity unto the elders of the city in the gate: And the damsel's father shall say unto the elders, I gave my daughter unto this man to wife, and he hateth her; And lo, he hath given occasions of speech against her, saying, I found not thy daughter a maid ... And they shall spread the cloth before the elders of the city. And the elders of that city shall take that man and chastise him ... But if this thing be true, and the tokens of virginity be not found for the damsel: Then shall they bring out the damsel to the door of her father's house, and the men of the city shall stone her with stones that she die: because she hath wrought folly in Israel, to play the whore in her father's house ...

Old Testament: Deuteronomy 22: 13–18, 20–1

If you should take your wife in adultery, you may with impunity put her to death without a trial; but if you should commit adultery or indecency, she must not presume to lay a finger on you, nor does the law allow it.

Cato the Elder (234–149 BC), Roman statesman and writer

There are only about twenty murders a year in London and many not at all serious – some are just husbands killing their wives.

Commander G. H. Hatherill, Scotland Yard, 1954

Though destitute of virtue or seeking pleasure elsewhere, or devoid of good qualities, a husband must be constantly worshipped as a god.

Laws of Manu, *Hindu text,* c. *200 BC–c. AD 200*

If a man avoids Marriage and all the troubles women bring
And never takes a wife, at last he comes
To a miserable old age, and does not have
Anyone to care for the old man.

Hesiod (eighth century BC), Greek epic poet

Wives are young men's mistresses, companions for middle age, and old men's nurses.

Francis Bacon (1561–1626), English philosopher, statesman and essayist, from Essays of Marriage and Single Life, 1597

I think women are basically quite lazy. Marriage is still a woman's best investment, because she can con some man into supporting her for the rest of his life.

Alan Whicker, British broadcaster and writer, Observer, 10 September 1972

Never trust a woman even if she has borne you seven children.

Japanese proverb

Man does not exist for the sake of woman, but woman exists for the sake of man and hence there shall be this difference, that a man shall love his wife, but never be subject to her, but the wife shall honour and fear the man.

Martin Luther (1483–1546), German religious reformer, from Vindication of Married Life

Powerful men often succeed through the help of their wives. Powerful women only succeed in spite of their husbands.

Linda Lee-Potter, British journalist, Daily Mail, *16 May 1984*

To marry a man out of pity is folly; and if you think you are going to influence the kind of fellow who has 'never had a chance, poor devil', you are profoundly mistaken. One can only influence the strong characters in life, not the weak; and it is the height of vanity to suppose that you can make an honest man of anyone.

Margot Asquith, Countess of Oxford and Asquith (1865–1945), political hostess and wit

Mrs Hall of Sherbourne was brought to bed yesterday of a dead child, some weeks before she expected, owing to a fright. I suppose she happened unawares to look at her husband.

Jane Austen (1775–1817), British novelist, letter, 27 October 1798

No man should marry until he has studied anatomy and dissected at least one woman.

Honoré de Balzac (1799–1850), French novelist, from La Physiologie du mariage

Courtship to marriage, as a very witty prologue to a very dull play.

William Congreve (1670–1729), British dramatist, from The Old Bachelor

Marriage is a wonderful invention; but then again, so is a bicycle-repair kit.

Billy Connolly, Scottish comedian and actor

Here lies my wife; here let her lie!
Now she's at rest, and so am I.

John Dryden (1631–1700), English poet, critic and dramatist

Non, j'aurai des maîtresses. (No, I shall have mistresses.)

King George II of Britain and Ireland (1683–1760), to Queen Caroline on her deathbed, on her suggesting that he should marry again when she was gone

A bachelor needs inspiration in order to seduce a woman, a married man only needs an excuse.

Helen Rowland (1875–1950), US writer and journalist

Men who have pierced ears are better prepared for marriage. They have experienced pain and bought jewellery.

Rita Rudner, US comedian

Men who write love letters don't live in this century.

Ibid.

Whenever you want to marry someone, go have lunch with his ex-wife.

Shelley Winters, US actress

Marriage is a great institution, but I'm not ready for an institution.

Mae West (1892–1980), US film actress

When a girl gets married she exchanges the attention of many men for the inattention of one.

Helen Rowland (1875–1950), US writer and journalist

My mother gave me this advice: trust your husband, adore your husband, and get as much as you can in your own name.

Joan Rivers, US comedian

Husbands are living proof that women have a sense of humour.

Anon.

Sometimes I wonder if men and women suit each other. Perhaps they should live next door and just visit now and then.

Katharine Hepburn, US actress

Don't marry a man to reform him – that's what reform schools are for.

Mae West (1892–1980), US film actress

My grandmother was a very tough woman. She buried three husbands. Two of them were just napping.

Rita Rudner, US comedian

Personally, I think if a woman hasn't met the right man by the time she's twenty-four, she may be lucky.

Jean Kerr, US playwright

Any intelligent woman who reads the marriage contract, and then goes into it, deserves all the consequences.

Isadora Duncan (1878–1927), US dancer

I require only three things of a man. He must be handsome, ruthless and stupid.

Dorothy Parker (1893–1967), US writer, poet, critic and wit

It is always incomprehensible to a man that a woman should refuse an offer of marriage.

Jane Austen (1775–1817), British novelist

Only time can heal your broken heart, just as time can heal his broken arms and legs.

Miss Piggy, US comedian and artiste

Any woman who still thinks marriage is a fifty-fifty proposition is only proving that she doesn't understand either men or percentages.

Florynce Kennedy, US writer

A man in love is incomplete until he has married. Then he's finished.

Zsa Zsa Gabor, Hungarian-born US film actress

Husbands are chiefly good lovers when they are betraying their wives.

Marilyn Monroe (1926–62), US film actress

Marriage to a lover is fatal; lovers are not husbands. More important, husbands are not lovers.

Carolyn Heilbrun, US educationalist

When two people marry they become in the eyes of the law one person, and that one person is the husband!

Shana Alexander, Introduction to US state-by-state guide to women's legal rights, 1975

Before marriage, a man will lie awake all night thinking about something you said; after marriage he'll fall asleep before you finish saying it.

Helen Rowland (1875–1950), US writer and journalist

Man long ago decided that woman's sphere was anything he did not wish to do himself, and as he did not particularly care for the straight and narrow way, he felt free to recommend it to women in general. He did not wish to tie himself too close to home either and still he knew somebody should stay on the job, so he decided that home was woman's sphere.

Nellie McClung (1895–1951), Canadian suffragist

Father had conversations. Mother took boarders.

Louisa May Alcott (1832–88), US novelist

You see an awful lot of smart guys with dumb women, but you hardly ever see a smart woman with a dumb guy.

Erica Jong, US writer

It seems the older the men get, the younger their new wives get.

Elizabeth Taylor, US film actress

These are hard times for men, for they are losing their servants.

Charlotte Perkins Gilman (1860–1935), US writer and feminist

MARRIAGE QUIPS

Is it all right to bring a girlfriend to the wedding?
Not if you are the groom.

How can you tell the married men at a wedding reception?
They're the ones dancing with everyone but their wives.

What do you call a woman who knows where her husband is every night?
A widow.

What is one thing that all men at singles bars have in common?
They are married.

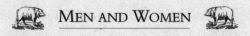

MEN AND WOMEN

A woman worries about the future until she gets a husband. A man never worries about the future until he gets a wife.

Married men live longer than single men – but married men are a lot more willing to die.

A woman marries a man expecting he will change, but he doesn't. A man marries a woman expecting that she won't change, and she does.

There are two times when a man doesn't understand a woman – before marriage and after marriage.

When reminiscing about weddings, women talk about the ceremony. Men talk about the stag night.

Husbands are like children – they're fine if they're someone else's.

The best reason to divorce a man is a health reason: you're sick of him.

 ## MEN'S REAL MEANINGS

Will you marry me?

Both my roommates have moved out, I can't find the washing machine, and there is no more peanut butter.

Honey, we don't need material things to prove our love.

I forgot our anniversary again.

You know I could never love anyone else.

I am used to the way you yell at me, and realize it could be worse.

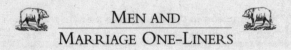

MEN AND
MARRIAGE ONE-LINERS

How do you keep your husband from reading your e-mail?
Rename the 'Mail' folder 'Instruction Manuals'.

A woman placed a personal ad. that read, 'Husband wanted'.
The next day she received hundreds of letters. They all said
the same thing: 'You can have mine!'

At a cocktail party, one woman said to another, 'Aren't you
wearing your wedding ring on the wrong finger?' The other
replied, 'Yes, I am – I married the wrong man.'

After a quarrel, a husband said to his wife, 'You know, I was
a fool when I married you.' The wife replied, 'Yes, dear, but
I was in love and didn't notice.'

What do you call a woman without an arsehole?
Divorced.

What's the difference between a man and childbirth?
*One is an almost unbearable pain and the other involves having
a baby.*

How can you tell if your husband is dead?

The sex is the same, but you get the remote control.

How is an ex-husband like an inflamed appendix?

It caused you a lot of pain, and after it was removed you found out you didn't need it anyway.

What do men and tights have in common?

They either cling, run or don't fit right in the crotch.

Why do men want to marry virgins?

They can't stand criticism.

Men are always whining about how we're suffocating them. Personally, I think if you can hear them whining, you're not pressing hard enough on the pillow!

What's the fastest way to a man's heart?

Through his chest with a sharp knife.

Losing a husband can be hard. In my case, it was damned near impossible.

Husband: 'Will you love me when I grow old and overweight?'
Wife: 'Yes I do.'

Why do female black widow spiders kill the male after mating?

To stop the snoring before it starts.

How are husbands like lawn mowers?

They're hard to get started, emit foul odours, and don't work half the time.

How do you scare a man?

Sneak up behind him and start throwing rice.

What do you do with a bachelor who thinks he's God's gift?

Exchange him.

Why do bachelors like smart women?

Opposites attract.

What's the difference between a husband and a boyfriend?

About forty-five minutes.

What do you do if your boyfriend walks out?

Shut the door.

Definition of a bachelor: a man who has missed the opportunity to make some woman miserable.

What's the difference between getting a divorce and getting circumcised?

When you get a divorce, you get rid of the whole prick.

There was a lady who said, 'I never knew what happiness was until I got married . . . and then it was too late.'

Marriage is not a word; it is a sentence.

What do you call a man who has lost 99 per cent of his brain?

A widower.

How do you grow your own dope?

Plant a man.

Man: 'I want to give myself to you.'
Woman: 'Sorry, I don't accept cheap gifts.'

What's the difference between a man and a lawn mower?

Lawnmowers don't bitch after they cut the grass.

Love is blind, but marriage is a real eye-opener.

Men are like high heels. They're easy to walk on once you get the hang of it.

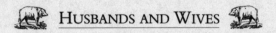 HUSBANDS AND WIVES

'I never would have married you if I knew how stupid you were,' shouted the woman to her husband.

He replied, 'You should've known how stupid I was the minute I asked you to marry me.'

'I got married,' said the first pub regular, 'So that I could have sex three, four or five times a week.'

'That's very ironic,' said the second regular. 'That's exactly why I got divorced.'

After a few years of being married, the wife surprised her husband with a new car, a ring and other wonderful gifts to celebrate their anniversary. When she asked what he had bought, he told her, a new sable coat, a vacation and a big surprise. With that he opened his robe and showed her that he had had the words 'I Love You' tattooed on his penis.

To which the wife replied, 'I don't care what you say, but don't try putting words in my mouth.'

'I was married three times,' explained the man to a newly discovered drinking partner, 'and I'll never marry again. My first two wives died of eating poison mushrooms and my third wife died of a fractured skull.'

'That's a shame,' said his friend. 'How did it happen?'

'She wouldn't eat the mushrooms.'

An old man goes to the Wizard to ask him if he can remove a curse he has been living with for the last forty years. The Wizard says, 'Maybe, but you will have to tell me the exact words that were used to put the curse on you.'

The old man says without hesitation, 'I now pronounce you man and wife.'

Young son: Is it true, Dad, that in some parts of Africa a man doesn't know his wife until he marries her?
Father: That happens in every country, son.

Ad. seen in paper:

FOR SALE BY OWNER

Complete set of Encyclopaedia Britannica. 45 volumes.
Excellent condition. £600 or best offer. No longer needed.
Got married last weekend. Wife knows everything.

Two drunks were in a pub sitting at the bar and staring into their drinks. One got a curious look on his face and asked, 'Hey, Pete! You ever seen an ice cube with a hole in it before?'

'Yep. I been married to one for fifteen years.'

'Congratulations my boy!' said the groom's uncle. 'I'm sure you'll look back and remember today as the happiest day of your life.'

'But I'm not getting married until tomorrow,' protested his nephew.

'I know,' replied the uncle. 'That's exactly what I mean.'

A husband stepped on one of those coin-operated scales that tell you your fortune and weight and dropped in a coin.

'Listen to this,' he said to his wife, showing her a small, white card. 'It says I'm energetic, bright, resourceful and a great lover.'

'Yeah,' his wife nodded, 'and it has your weight wrong, too.'

'Are you and Mike serious?' a girl asked her friend while they were talking over cocktails. 'We're still a little short of a meeting of the minds,' she replied. 'I want a big, old-fashioned June wedding, and he wants a quickie in the back seat.'

'I must take every precaution not to get pregnant,' said Jane to Susan.

'But I thought you said your hubby had a vasectomy,' Susan responded.

'He did. That's why I have to take every precaution.'

The Smiths were dining out when his wife noticed a familiar face at the bar.

'Honey,' she said as she pointed the guy out, 'That guy at the bar has been drinking like that since I left him seven years ago.'

Her husband said, 'That's silly, no one celebrates that much!'

Some time after their bitter divorce, a man happened to pull up beside his ex-wife at a traffic signal. He shouted over, 'So . . . out looking for a little, huh?'

She smiled sweetly and said, 'No, I had six years of that with you. Now, I'm out looking for a LOT!'

Worried about their less than exciting sex life, a young wife sent her husband to a therapist who wound up treating him with self-hypnosis. And, to her joy, everything got much better.

However, she could not help but notice that each night, early into their lovemaking, the husband would dash out to the bathroom for several minutes. This tormented her until finally, one night, she followed him.

There, in front of the mirror, she found him applying his newly learned therapeutic technique: 'She's not my wife ... She's not my wife ... She's not my wife ... '

One evening, after a discussion during a Social Studies lesson, my brother asked my dad, 'Why isn't a man allowed to have more than one wife?'

My dad's answer earned him a laugh from my brother – and a night on the couch: 'Because the law protects those who are incapable of protecting themselves.'

Rex's barn burned down and his wife, Susan, called the insurance company. Susan told the insurance company, 'We had that barn insured for fifty thousand and I want my money.'

The agent replied, 'Whoa there, just a minute, Susan. Insurance doesn't work quite like that. We will ascertain the value of what was insured and provide you with a new one of comparable worth.'

There was a long pause before Susan replied, 'Then I'd like to cancel the policy on my husband.'

Overheard: 'Has your husband lived up to all the things he said before you were married?'

'No, He's only lived up to one of them.'

'Which one was that?'

'He said he wasn't good enough for me.'

Once upon a time, a beautiful, independent, self-assured princess happened upon a frog in a pond. The frog said to the princess, 'I was once a handsome prince until an evil witch put a spell on me. One kiss from you and I will turn back into a prince and then we can marry, move in to the castle with my mum, and you can hold down a full-time job, prepare my meals, clean my clothes, bear my children and forever feel happy doing so.'

That night, the princess dined happily on frog's legs.

A man and his wife had a bitter quarrel on the day of their wedding anniversary. Infuriated, the husband decided to give his wife a tombstone, telling the mason that he wanted it to have the inscription: 'Here lies my wife . . . cold as ever!'

Later his livid wife bought a return present, a tombstone with the inscription: 'Here lies my husband . . . stiff at last!'

One evening a wife drew her husband's attention to the couple next door and said, 'Do you see that couple? How devoted they are? He kisses her every time they meet. Why don't you do that?'

'I would love to,' replied the husband, 'But I don't know her well enough.'

A man was trying to console a friend who'd just found his wife in bed with another man. 'Get over it mate,' he said. 'It's not the end of the world.'

'It's all right for you to say,' answered his friend. 'But what if you came home one night and caught another man in bed with your wife?'

The man thought for a moment, then said, 'I'd break his white stick and kick his guide dog in the arse.'

A priest and a nun were lost in a snowstorm. After a while, they came upon a small cabin. Being exhausted, they prepared to go to sleep. There was a stack of blankets and a sleeping bag on the floor but only one bed. Being a gentleman, the priest said, 'Sister, you sleep on the bed. I'll sleep on the floor in the sleeping bag.'

Just as he got zipped up in the bag and was beginning to fall asleep, the nun said, 'Father, I'm cold.'

He unzipped the sleeping bag, got up, got a blanket from the pile and laid it over her. Then he got back into the sleeping bag, zipped it up, and was just starting to drift off to sleep when the nun once again said, 'Father, I'm still very cold.'

He unzipped the bag, got up again, put another blanket on her and got into the sleeping bag once more.

Just as his eyes closed, she said, 'Father, I'm sooooo cold.'

This time, he remained where he was. Then he said, 'Sister, I have an idea. We're out here in the wilderness where no one will ever know what happened. Let's pretend we're married.'

The nun said, 'That's fine by me.'

To which the priest yelled out, 'Get up and get your own stupid blanket!'

3 THE PIG BANG THEORY

men and sex

If men were as great lovers as they think they are, we women wouldn't have time to do our hair.

Marlene Dietrich, German actress and singer

It's not the men in my life that counts, it's the life in my men.

Mae West (1892–1980), US film actress

The centre of this case, members of the jury, is Clodia, a noble and notorious woman. I shall not say more about her than I must to deny the charges. As a barrister, I must drive back those who lead the attack. And I would do it more violently if I were not ill-disposed towards her 'lover' – sorry, 'brother' – Clodius (I'm always making that mistake!). I'll go easy on her ... I don't think it is right to lay into a woman (especially one ... who enjoys a good lay with all and sundry . . .) Suppose a woman, quite unlike Clodia, of course, were available to everyone, who always had her latest boyfriend hanging round, who always provided open house for every man and had an open purse for every young man with a mean father; someone who was a widow without restrictions living with gay abandon, extravagantly and promiscuously; you would hardly call someone who associated with a woman like that an adulterer, now would you?

Cicero (103–43 BC), Roman consul, orator and writer, from Pro Caelio

Men are those creatures with two legs and eight hands.

Jayne Mansfield (1932–67), US film actress

Men only call themselves feminists in the hope of getting a more intelligent fuck.

Kathy Lette, Australian feminist novelist

A woman is a woman until the day she dies, but a man's a man only as long as he can.

Jackie 'Moms' Mabley (1894–1975), US singer and comedian

I sometimes think that what men really want now is a sexually experienced virgin.

Anon.

Give a man a free hand and he'll run it all over you.

Mae West (1892–1980), US film actress

Possibly he is also gay; it's hard for her to tell with literate Englishmen. Some days they all seem gay to her, other days they all seem not gay. Flirtation is no clue, because Englishmen of this class will flirt with anything. She's noticed this before. They will flirt with dogs if nothing else is handy.

Margaret Atwood, Canadian poet and novelist, from Wilderness Tips

Prostitutes for pleasure, concubines for service, wives for breeding and a melon for ecstasy.

Attributed to Sir Richard Burton (1821–90), British explorer, writer and translator

When this judge let a rapist go because the woman had been wearing a miniskirt and so was 'asking for it' I thought, ladies, what we all should do is this: next time we see an ugly guy on the street, shoot him. After all, he knew he was ugly when he left the house. He was asking for it.

Ellen Cleghorn, US writer and comedian

Whosoever shall lie in sexual intercourse with a woman who has an issue of blood; either out of the ordinary course or at the usual period, does no better deed than if he should burn the corpse of his own son, born of his own body, and killed by a spear, and drop its fat into the fire.

Fargard, Zoroastrian text, c. tenth century AD

However, rape is a perfectly natural function. It means that a man so desires a woman that he takes her by force. Since a man is much stronger than a woman it does not necessarily involve much violence, and in many cases the woman duly submits.

Professor J. M. V. Browner, Vive la Différence, 1981

Women who say no do not always mean no. It is not just a question of saying no, it is a question of how she says it, how she shows and makes it clear. If she doesn't want it she only has to keep her legs shut and she would not get it without force and there would be marks of force being used.

His Honour Judge (David) Wild, British circuit judge, Cambridge, 1982

What they love to yield
They would often rather have stolen. Rough
Seduction
Delights them, the boldness of near rape
Is a compliment.

Ovid (43 BC – ?AD 17), Roman poet, from The Art of Love

She burns and as it were, dries up the semen received by her from the male, and if by chance a child is conceived it is ill-formed and does not remain nine months in the mother's womb.

John Davenport, describing the result of orgasm in women, from Curiositates Eroticae Phisiologiae, 1875

Older women are best because they always think they may
be doing it for the last time.

Ian Fleming (1908–64), British novelist

My brain: it's my second favourite organ.

Woody Allen, US film maker and actor, from Sleeper

Gentlemen always seem to remember blondes.

Anita Loos (1891–1981), US novelist, from Gentlemen Prefer Blondes

In high school and college my sister Mary was very popular
with the boys, but I had braces on my teeth and got high
marks.

Betty MacDonald (1908–1958), US writer, from The Egg and I

Men seldom make passes
At girls who wear glasses.

Dorothy Parker (1893–1967), US writer, poet, critic and wit

'Easy' is an adjective used to describe a woman who has the
sexual morals of a man.

Nancy Linn-Desmond

So many men, and so many reasons not to sleep with any of
them.

Anon.

Never refer to any part of his body below the waist as 'cute' or 'little'; never expect him to do anything about birth control; never ask if he changes his sheets seasonally; never request that he sleep in the wet spot.

C. E. Crimmins

If I was the Virgin Mary, I would have said no.

Stevie Smith (1902–71), British poet

Sometimes it is less hard to wake up feeling lonely when you are alone than to wake up feeling lonely when you are with someone.

Liv Ullmann, Swedish film actress

If a man is highly sexed he's virile. If a woman is, she's a nymphomaniac. With them it's power but with us it's a disease! Even the act of sex is called penetration! Why don't they call it enclosure?

Gemma Hatchback

Thou shalt not rape was conspicuously missing from the Ten Commandments.

Susan Brownmiller, US writer

The average girl would rather have beauty than brains because she knows that the average man can see much better than he can think.

Ladies' Home Journal, 1947

The act of sex . . . is man's last desperate stand at super-intendency.

Bette Davis (1908–89), US film actress

The problem is, they have too many hormones. And they have this trouble all the time, not just ten days a month, like a woman does.

Sally Dustin, from a letter in MS magazine

The only place men want depth in a woman is in her décolletage.

Zsa Zsa Gabor, Hungarian-born US film actress

For men obsessed with women's underwear, a course in washing, ironing and mending is recommended.

Charlotte Perkins Gilman (1860–1935), US writer and feminist

I'm not going to hang myself just because some wretched little man sticks his dick in me.

Germaine Greer, Australian feminist and writer, of the experience of being raped

All too many men still seem to believe, in a rather naive and egocentric way, that what feels good to them is automatically what feels good to a woman.

Shere Hite, US writer

If men knew what women laughed about, they would never sleep with us.

Erica Jong, US writer

A hard man is good to find.

Mae West (1892–1980), US film actress

Some men are all right in their places — if only they knew the right places!

Ibid.

When man was first created, he was given only twenty years of normal sex life. Naturally, he was horrified. Only twenty years!

The monkey also was given twenty years, but said that ten years was plenty. The man asked for the monkey's other ten years and they were given to him.

The lion was also given twenty years, but he also said he only needed ten years. Again, the man asked for the other ten years, and the lion agreed.

Then came the donkey, and he was also given twenty years, but like the other animals, ten years was enough for him. And again, man asked for, and was given, ten more years.

Now, this explains why man today has twenty years of normal sex life, then ten years of monkeying around, ten years of lion about it and last of all, ten years of making an ass of himself.

MEN AND SEX ONE-LINERS

Man: 'If I could just see you naked, I'd die happy.'
Woman: 'Yeah, but if I saw you naked, I'd probably die laughing.'

Why do so many women fake orgasms?

Because so many men fake foreplay.

Why do men tend to name their penises?

They want to be on a first-name basis with anything that makes 95 per cent of their decisions for them.

Husband: 'Want a quickie?'
Wife: 'As opposed to what?'

When you want a man to play with you, wear a full-length black nightgown with buttons all over it. Sure it's uncomfortable, but it makes you look just like his remote control.

What have men and floor tiles got in common?

If you lay them properly the first time, you can walk all over them for life.

Why is sleeping with a man like a soap opera?
Just when it's getting interesting, they're finished until next time.

Why do men like masturbation?
It's sex with someone they love.

What's the definition of a male chauvinist pig?
A man who hates every bone in a woman's body, except his own.

Why did the man cross the road?
He heard the chicken was a slut.

Why don't women blink during foreplay?
They don't have time.

What is the best way to annoy your wife during sex?
Call her on the telephone.

Why do women pay more attention to their appearance
than improving their minds?
Because most men are stupid, but few are blind.

How are men like vacations?
They never seem to be long enough!

Why are men like popcorn?
They satisfy you, but only for a little while.

Why are men and spray paint alike?
One squeeze and they're all over you.

What is the definition of 'making love'?
Something a woman does while a guy is screwing her.

What's the difference between a pregnant woman and a man?
One has morning sickness, the other has morning stiffness.

The main point of having a boyfriend is so that he can one day graduate to the exalted status of a 'former boyfriend.'

How do men exercise on the beach?
By sucking in their stomachs every time a bikini goes by.

What do you call a man who expects to have sex on the second date?
Slow.

What's a man's definition of a romantic evening?
Sex.

Why do men have legs?
So their brains don't drag on the ground.

Why were men given larger brains than dogs?
So they wouldn't hump women's legs at cocktail parties.

Men are like copiers. You need them for reproduction, but that's about it.

What can a bird do that a man can't?
Whistle through his pecker.

Women prefer thirty to forty-five minutes of foreplay. Men prefer thirty to forty-five seconds of foreplay. Men consider driving back to her place as part of the foreplay.

How can you tell if a man is sexually excited?
He's breathing.

A construction worker came home just in time to find his wife in bed with another man. So he dragged the man down the stairs to the garage and put his penis in a vice. He secured it tightly and removed the handle. Then he picked up a hacksaw.

The man, terrified, screamed, 'STOP! STOP! You're not going to cut it off, are you?'

The husband said, with a gleam of revenge in his eye, 'Nope. You are. I'm going to set the garage on fire.'

A guy came home from work, 'Honey, where are you?'

'I'm upstairs douching,' his wife answered.

'I told you never to talk like that!' he yelled.

'What do you want,' she called out, 'good grammar or good taste?'

A cowboy and his new bride ask the hotel desk clerk for a room. 'Congratulations on your wedding!' the clerk says. 'Would you like the bridal, then?'

'Naw, thanks,' says the cowboy. 'I'll just hold her by the ears till she gets the hang of it.'

The morning after their honeymoon, the wife says to her husband, 'You know, you're a really lousy lover.'

The husband replies, 'How would you know after only thirty seconds?'

4 TROUGH MIXTURE

*men and food and drink; men and shopping;
men as parents; men as travellers*

A man is in general better pleased when he has a good dinner upon his table, than when his wife talks Greek.

Samuel Johnson (1709–84), British writer, critic, lexicographer and conversationalist

It is an undoubted fact that meat spoils when touched by menstruating women.

British Medical Journal, *1878*

Women in Africa work like beasts of burden, fetching firewood, carrying water, looking after the children and growing food. They are Africa's main food producers but have little time to devote to the task. Often they are not legally regarded as adults; they frequently have no land rights; and a husband can keep his wife's earnings.

New Internationalist, June 1990

When Jimmy Thomas, Labour MP and cabinet minister in the 1920s, was asked whether his wife would be accompanying him on an official trip to Paris, he replied: 'You don't take a ham sandwich to the Lord Mayor's Banquet, do you?'

Not one man who drinks beer in a beer commercial has a beer belly.

Rita Rudner, US comedian

Never eat more than you can lift.

Miss Piggy, US comedian and artiste

My husband will cook, but not 'cook, cook'. He'll only barbecue. Men will cook as long as there's danger involved.

Rita Rudner, US comedian

Men just want their vittles and a lot they care who gives it to them.

Nellie McClung (1873–1951), Canadian suffragist

Most men cannot find in their own kitchen what most women can find in a stranger's kitchen.

Letty Cottin Pogrebin, US feminist writer

When men cook, cooking is viewed as an important activity; when women cook, it is just a household chore.

Margaret Mead (1901–78), US anthropologist and writer

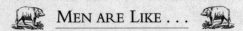

MEN ARE LIKE . . .

Men are like place mats. They only show up when there's food on the table.

Men are like chocolate bars. Sweet, smooth, and they usually head right for your hips.

Why are married women heavier than single women?

Single women come home, see what's in the fridge and go to bed. Married women come home, see what's in bed and go to the fridge.

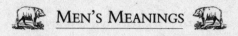

MEN'S MEANINGS

Can I help with dinner?   *Why isn't it already on the table?*

She's one of those rabid feminists.   *She refused to make my coffee.*

If you think the way to a man's heart is through his stomach you're aiming too high.

What food describes most men?
  Jerky.

What's a man's idea of a perfect date?
  A woman who answers the door stark naked holding a case of beer.

Why is food better than men?
  Because you don't have to wait an hour for seconds.

What is the difference between men and pigs?
  Pigs don't turn into men when they drink.

How is Colonel Sanders like the typical male?
  All he's concerned with is legs, breasts and thighs.

What do men and beer bottles have in common.
  They are both empty from the neck up.

A dietician was once addressing a large audience in Chicago. 'The material we put into our stomachs is enough to have killed most of us sitting here years ago. Red meat is awful. Vegetables can be disastrous, and none of us realizes what germs there are in our drinking water. But there is one thing that is the most dangerous of all, and all of us eat it. Can anyone here tell me what lethal product I'm referring to? You, sir, in the first row, please give us your idea.'

The man lowered his head and said, 'Wedding cake?'

The angry wife met her husband at the door. There was alcohol on his breath, and lipstick on his cheek. 'I assume,' she snarled, 'that there is a very good reason for you to come waltzing in at six o'clock in the morning!'

'There is,' he replied. 'Breakfast.'

A young couple, married just a few weeks, return from their honeymoon to face the beginning of their new lives. The next morning the husband wakes up, showers, dresses and makes his way to the kitchen where he finds his new wife crying.

So the husband inquires, 'What's wrong, honey?'

'Well, I came down here this morning to surprise you with a big breakfast, but I can't cook or clean.'

The husband smiles his biggest smile and says, 'There, there, sweetie! I don't care that you can't cook and clean. Come on up to the bedroom and I'll show you what I'd like for breakfast.'

So off they went to the bedroom.

That afternoon, the husband comes home for lunch to find his new wife crying again in the kitchen. 'What's wrong now, sweetie?'

'Well, the same thing as this morning. I came in here to make you something for lunch and I just can't cook.'

Again the husband smiles and says, 'Why don't you come back up to the bedroom and I'll have my lunch there!'

So off they went to the bedroom again.

That evening the new husband comes home, walks in the house and sees his new bride sliding, stark naked, down the banisters of the stairs. Up she runs, and WHOOSH! – down the banisters again.

After the third trip the husband asks, 'What are you doing, honey?'

'Warming up your supper!' she replies.

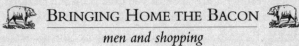

BRINGING HOME THE BACON
men and shopping

Beware of the man who picks your dresses; he wants to wear them.

Erica Jong, US writer

When a man opens the car door for his wife, it's either a new car or a new wife.

HRH Prince Philip, Duke of Edinburgh, March 1988

How men hate waiting while their wives shop for clothes and trinkets; how women hate waiting, often for much of their lives, while their husbands shop for fame and glory.

Thomas Szasz, US psychiatrist

Most men hate to shop. That's why in department stores the men's department is usually on the ground floor, two inches from the door.

Rita Rudner, US comedian

The only difference between men and boys is the price of their toys.

Anon.

How does a man show that he is planning for the future?
He buys two cases of beer.

What do you instantly know about a well-dressed man?
His wife is good at picking out clothes.

 MEN'S MEANINGS

I was just thinking about you, and got you these roses.

The girl selling them on the corner was really sexy.

You look terrific.

Oh God, please don't try on one more outfit – I'm starving.

A man walks into a supermarket and buys :
  one bar of soap
  one toothbrush
  one tube of toothpaste
  one loaf of bread
  one pint of milk
  one single-serving carton of cereal
  one single-serving frozen dinner

The girl at the checkout looks at him and says, 'You're single, aren't you?'

  The man replies, very sarcastically, 'How did you guess?'

  'Because you're so damn ugly!' she ripostes.

A man parked his car at the supermarket and was walking past an empty trolley when he heard a woman ask, 'Excuse me, did you want that trolley?'

  'No,' he answered, 'I'm only after one thing.'

  As he walked toward the store, he heard her murmur, 'Typical male.'

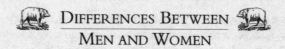

DIFFERENCES BETWEEN
MEN AND WOMEN

Groceries

A woman makes a list of things she needs and then goes to the store and buys these things.

A man waits until the only items left in his fridge are half of a lemon, and something turning green. Then he goes grocery shopping. He buys everything that looks good. By the time he reaches the checkout counter, his cart is packed tighter than a street-market stall. Of course, this will not stop him from going to the ten-items-or-less lane.

Menopause

When a woman reaches menopause, she goes through a variety of complicated emotional, psychological, and biological changes. The nature and degree of the changes vary with the individual.

Menopause in a man provokes a uniform reaction. He buys aviator glasses, a snazzy French cap, leather driving gloves, and goes shopping for an expensive sports car.

Toys

Little girls love to play with toys. Then, when they reach the age of eleven or twelve, they lose interest.

Men never grow out of their obsession with toys. As they get older, their toys simply become more expensive and impractical. Examples of men's toys: miniature TVs, car phones, complicated juicers and blenders, graphic equalizers, small robots that serve cocktails on command, video games, and anything that blinks, beeps and requires at least six batteries to operate.

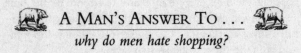

A MAN'S ANSWER TO . . .

why do men hate shopping?

It's an evolutionary thing. Men hunt. Women gather. We just want to go out, kill it, and bring it back. Who wants to spend hours and hours to look at things we have no intention of killing? Er . . . buying?

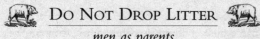

DO NOT DROP LITTER
men as parents

If – and good luck to you – you have a baby and it is male,
let it live; but if it is female, expose it.

Papyrus fragment of a letter from Egypt, first century AD

The mother of the child that is called hers is not really
its parent. She just nurses the seed that is planted within
her by the child's true parent, the male . . . and if you want
proof of what I say, here it is: here is Athene, child of Zeus,
who was born with no help from a mother's womb; she is
living proof that the male can father a child with no help
from a female.

Aeschylus (525–456 BC), Greek tragic dramatist, from the Eumenides

The only time a woman really succeeds in changing a man
is when he's a baby.

Natalie Wood (1938–81), US film actress

Men will now get up and walk with the baby in the
middle of the night, change its nappies and give it
a bottle, but in their heart of hearts they still think they
shouldn't have to.

Rita Rudner, US comedian

A man in a delivery room is about as helpful as a nun at a bar-mitzvah.

Ibid.

Men name their children after themselves, women don't. Have you ever met a Sally, Jr?

Ibid.

Father asked us what was God's noblest work. Anna said men but I said babies. Men are often bad; babies never are.

Louisa May Alcott (1832–1888), US novelist

Inside every adult male is a denied little boy.

Nancy Friday, US writer

The failure of men to cultivate their capacity for listening has a profound impact on their capacity for parenting, for it is mothers more than fathers who are most likely to still their own voices so they may hear and draw out the voices of their children.

Mary Field Belenky, Blythe McVicar Clinchy, Nancy Rule Goldberger and Jill Mattuck Tarule, US writers

If it were natural for fathers to care for their sons, they would not need so many laws commanding them to do so.

Phyllis Chesler, US psychiatrist

Divorced men are now more likely to meet their car payments than their child-support obligations.

Susan Faludi, US journalist

Only men could be responsible for the belief that a boy child is to be preferred to a girl child.

Margaret Fuller (1810–50), US feminist

If men had to bear babies, there'd never be more than one child in a family. And he'd be a boy.

Clare Boothe Luce (1903–87), US writer, playwright, journalist, politician and diplomat

Of course my father always said I should have grown up to be a boy.

Maria Goeppert Mayer (1906–1972), US physicist

The thing to remember about fathers is, they're men.

Phyllis McGinley (1905–78), US poet

Men do not want to have to take care of children. Rule them, yes. Play with them, yes. Take credit for their achievements, certainly. But not care for their bottles, diapers, mess, spills, tears, tantrums, laundry, lunches, nightmares, and the million daily details of childhood.

Letty Cottin Pogrebin, US feminist writer

A man might have a harem if he chose, and if he could defend it, but the concept of 'my' son requires the woman to be monogamous.

Reay Tannahill, US writer

Fathers are present as absences in family life. Who really had a father? Even people who did have fathers didn't. Men were working.

Mona Simpson, US writer

Have you ever wondered why there are so many men in the 'right-to-life' movement and so few in child-care?

Letty Cottin Pogrebin, US feminist writer

Common is the man who will permit his aged mother to carry pails of water and armfuls of wood, or his wife to lug a twenty-pound baby, hour after hour, without ever offering to relieve her.

Elisabeth Cady Stanton (1815–1902), US suffragist

A woman knows all about her children. She knows about dentist appointments and soccer games and romances and best friends and favourite foods and secret fears and hopes and dreams.

A man is vaguely aware of some short people living in the house.

Anon.

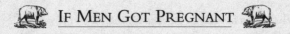 IF MEN GOT PREGNANT

Maternity leave would last two years . . . with full pay.

There'd be a cure for stretch marks.

Natural childbirth would become obsolete.

Morning sickness would rank as the nation's number-one health problem.

All methods of birth control would be improved to 100 per cent effectiveness.

Children would be kept in the hospital until they were toilet trained.

They'd have to stop saying, 'I'm afraid I'll drop him.'

There would be drive-in abortions.

Paternity suits would be a line of clothes.

They'd stay in bed for the entire nine months.

Menus at most restaurants would list ice cream and pickles as entrées.

Why do doctors slap babies' bottoms right after they're born?

To knock the penises off the smart ones.

Why is psychoanalysis quicker for men than for women?

When it's time to go back to childhood, he's already there.

What do electric trains and breasts have in common?

They're intended for children, but it's usually the men who end up playing with them.

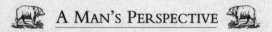

A MAN'S PERSPECTIVE

One night a wife found her husband standing over their newborn baby's cot. Silently she watched him. As he stood looking down at the sleeping infant, she saw on his face a mixture of emotions: disbelief, doubt, delight, amazement, enchantment, scepticism. Touched by this unusual display and the deep emotions it aroused, with eyes glistening she slipped her arms around her husband.

'A penny for your thoughts,' she whispered in his ear.

'It's amazing!' he replied. 'I just can't see how anybody can make a cot like that for only £29.99!'

THE WORLD ATLAS OF SWINE

men as travellers

If they can put one man on the moon, why can't they put them all?

Anon.

Don't accept rides from strange men, and remember that all men are strange as hell.

Robin Morgan, US writer and poet

He never gets lost. It's always my fault. I've read the map wrong. Or I've written down the wrong directions. Or distracted him when he was supposed to make a turn.

US housewife, New Jersey

If we go away, even for a weekend, he forgets to pack his underwear, but he's brought a suitcase full of work.

US housewife, Georgia

I am *not* lost. I know exactly where we are.

I'm lost. I have no idea where we are, and no one will ever see us alive again.

Why did the tribes in Israel wander the desert for forty years?

Because even back then, men wouldn't stop to ask directions.

If a woman is out driving and she finds herself in unfamiliar surroundings, she will stop at a petrol station and ask for directions.

Men consider this to be a sign of weakness. A man will never stop and ask for directions. Men will drive in a circle for hours, all the while saying things like, 'Looks like I've found a new way to get there,' and, 'I know I'm in the neighbourhood. I recognize that Esso garage.'

5 HOGGING THE LIMELIGHT

tendency of men to garner praise for themselves and apportion blame to others; men as paralysing boars; hypochondria of men; men and money and work

In passing, I would like to say that the first time Adam had a chance he laid the blame on woman.

Nancy, Lady Astor (1879–1964), British politician

Behind almost every woman you ever heard of stands a man who let her down.

Naomi Bliven, US writer

Both men and women are fallible. The difference is, women know it.

Eleanor Bron, British actress

If there's anything disagreeable going on, men are sure to get out of it.

Jane Austen (1775–1817), British novelist, from Northanger Abbey

Gentlemen: when you 'come down' to commonplace or small talk with an intelligent lady, one of two things is the consequence: she either recognizes the condescension and despises you, or else she accepts it as the highest intellectual effort of which you are capable, and rates you accordingly.

Mrs E. B. Duffey, from The Ladies' and Gentlemen's Etiquette, 1877

The hen knows when it is daybreak but allows the rooster to make the announcement.

Ashanti proverb

And do you not know that you are an Eve? The sentence of God on this sex of yours lives in this age: the guilt must of necessity live too. You are the devil's gateway: you are the unsealer of that tree: you are the first deserter of the divine law: you are she who persuaded him whom the devil was not valiant enough to attack. You destroyed so easily God's image, man. On account of your desert – that is, death – even the Son of God had to die.

Tertullian (AD ?160–?225), Carthaginian father of the Church

My nose is huge! Vile snub-nose, flat-nosed ass, flat-head, let me inform you that I am proud of such an appendage, since a big nose is the proper sign of a friendly, good, courteous, witty, liberal, and brave man, such as I am.

Edmond Rostand (1868–1918), French poet and dramatist, from Cyrano de Bergerac

Women have served all these centuries as looking-glasses possessing the magic and delicious power of reflecting the figure of a man at twice its natural size.

Virginia Woolf (1882–1941), British novelist and critic, from A Room of One's Own

All men think that they're nice guys. Some are not. Contact me for a list.

Rita Rudner, US comedian

The people I'm furious with are the women's liberationists. They keep getting up on soap boxes and proclaiming that women are brighter than men. It's true, but it should be kept quiet or it ruins the whole racket.

Anita Loos (1893–1981), US novelist

If you're in a car with a man and he stops and asks some-one for directions, listen carefully, because he won't, and it will be your fault if you get lost.

Rita Rudner, US comedian

Men always think they're the best thing that's ever happened to you.

Ibid.

Why are women so much more interesting to men than men are to women?

Virginia Woolf (1882–1941), British novelist and critic

The earliest Chinese ideograph for 'male' was also a synonym for selfish.

Barbara G. Walker, US feminist writer

Dear Sirs,

Man to man, manpower, craftsman, working men, thinking man, the man in the street, fellow countrymen, the history of mankind, one-man show, man in his wisdom, statesman, forefathers, masterful, masterpiece, old masters, the brother-hood of man, Liberty, Equality, Fraternity, sons of free men, faith of our fathers, God the Father, God the Son, yours fraternally, amen.

Words fail me.

Stephanie Dowrick

The male ego with few exceptions is elephantine to start with.

Bette Davis (1908–89), US film actress

Men know everything – all of them – all the time – no matter how stupid or inexperienced or arrogant or ignorant they are.

Andrea Dworkin, US feminist

Men have convinced women to remain backstage so that only they have the limelight – and then they have dared to assert that their presence front stage proves their superiority and its divine origin!

Dale Spender, Australian feminist writer

Men interrupt women.

Deborah Tannen, US sociologist

Men frequently annoy women by usurping or switching the topic.

Ibid.

Any student of history knows that it is the story of men.

Kathryn Weibel, US writer

Show me a woman who doesn't feel guilty and I'll show you a man.

Erica Jong, US writer

Macho does not prove mucho.

Zsa Zsa Gabor, Hungarian-born US film actress

Men are unable to admit they are wrong, no matter how
lightweight the issue.

Sonia Friedman, US writer

 **MANSPEAK**

It would take too long   *I have no idea how it works.*
to explain.

Never trust a man who says he's the boss at home. He
probably lies about other things, too.

Men are like horoscopes. They always tell you what to do
and are usually wrong.

Women will sometimes admit making a mistake. The last
man who admitted that he was wrong was General Custer.

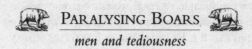

PARALYSING BOARS
men and tediousness

There is a moment when a man develops enough confidence in a relationship to bore you to death.

Eve Babitz

He's the kind of bore who's here today and here tomorrow.

Binnie Barnes

She had been bored all the afternoon by Percy Gryce – the mere thought seemed to waken an echo of his droning voice – but she could not ignore him on the morrow, she must follow up her success, must submit to more boredom, must be ready with fresh compliances and adaptabilities, and all on the bare chance that he might ultimately decide to do her the honour of boring her for life.

Edith Wharton (1862–1937), US novelist and short-story writer, from The House of Mirth

Roland has the inner life of a tree, or possibly of a stump.

Margaret Atwood, Canadian poet and novelist, from Wilderness Tips

One would wish for every girl who is growing up to womanhood that it might be brought home to her by some refined and ethically minded member of her own sex how insufferable a person woman becomes when, like a spoilt child, she exploits the indulgence of man; when she proclaims that it is his duty to serve her and to share with her his power and possessions; when she makes an outcry when he refuses to part with what is his own; and when she insists upon thrusting her society upon men everywhere.

Almroth Edward Wright (1861–1947), British bacteriologist

Men are always ready to respect anything that bores them.

Marilyn Monroe (1926–62), US film actress

One cannot be always laughing at a man without now and then stumbling on something witty.

Jane Austen (1775–1817), British novelist

If you talk about yourself, he'll think you're boring. If you talk about others he'll think you're a gossip. If you talk about him, he'll think you're a brilliant conversationalist.

Linda Sunshine

Women want mediocre men, and men are working hard to be as mediocre as possible.

Margaret Mead (1901–78), US anthropologist and writer

LAST SWILL AND TESTAMENT
hypochondria of men

Hungry Joe collected lists of fatal diseases and arranged them in alphabetical order so that he could put his finger without delay on any one he wanted to worry about.

Joseph Heller, US novelist, from Catch 22

How sickness enlarges the dimensions of a man's self to himself.

Charles Lamb (1775–1834), British essayist

Oh, don't fuss. I just cut myself, it's no big deal.

I have severed a limb, but will bleed to death before I admit I'm hurt.

When a concerned wife called him at home for the third time, the doctor lost his patience. 'There isn't a damn thing wrong with your husband,' he said. 'I've checked him out thoroughly and he only thinks he's sick.'

A week later the woman ran into the physician on the street. 'How's your husband?' he asked.

'Terrible,' the woman replied. 'Now he thinks he's dead.'

LAUGHING ALL THE WAY
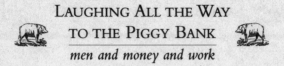
TO THE PIGGY BANK
men and money and work

Whatever women do they must do twice as well as men to be thought half as good. Luckily this is not difficult.

Charlotte Whitton

The law expressly forbids children and women from being able to make a contract about anything worth more than a bushel of barley.

Isæus (c.420– c.350 BC), Greek speech writer

A starving artist marrying a rich woman will not demand a pre-nuptial.

Rita Rudner, US comedian

Older men are not more mature. They just have more money ... which makes them appear more mature.

Ibid.

Rich men are often the stingiest. I had one rich boyfriend.
When we went out to dinner, I used to order lobster just to
watch his pupils constrict.

Ibid.

If you like easygoing, monogamous men, stay away from
billionaires.

Ibid.

The woman's position in the world today is so much harder
than a man's that it makes me choke every time I hear a man
complain about anything.

Katharine Hepburn, US actress

Whether he admits it or not, a man has been brought up to
look at money as a sign of his virility, a symbol of his power,
a bigger phallic symbol than a Porsche.

Victoria Billings, US writer

Men are men and women are women and their pay
cheques are just further evidence of their vast
biological differences, the powerful influence of the X
and Y chromosomes.

Mary Kay Blakely, US writer

Men are not opposed to women working, just against their being paid for it.

Barbara Bodichon (1827–91), British feminist writer

The fact that most gynaecologists are males is itself a colossal comment on 'our' society.

Mary Daly, US philosopher

The power of money is a distinctly male power. Money speaks, but it speaks with a male voice.

Andrea Dworkin, US feminist

'We men are the breadwinners,' say the sentimentalists, who are ashamed of their female relatives appearing to work, though female earnings usually drop into men's pockets.

Englishwoman's Journal, 1858

Men own 99 per cent of the world's property and earn 90 per cent of its wages, while producing only 55 per cent of the world's food and performing only one-third of the world's work.

Statistics taken from an international labour organization study presented at the United Nations Women's Conference in Copenhagen, 1980

Automation and unions have led to a continuously shortened day for men but the workday of housewives with children has remained constant.

Beverly Jones, US writer

Chances are better than even that if you ask the nearest man, he'll cheerfully tell you that housework is not work.

Penney Kome, Canadian journalist

Nine times out of ten when a man is altruistic it's a tax dodge.

Irma Kurtz, US-born British journalist

Never mind how many women are out there working. The workplace is still, for the most part, owned and run by men, and we're there because they've allowed us to be there – sometimes because they had to – and we know it and they know it and they know we know it.

Betty Rollin, US writer

If men can run the world, why can't they stop wearing neckties? How intelligent is it to start the day by tying a little noose around your neck?

Linda Ellerbee, US broadcaster

One of the things being in politics has taught me is that men are not a reasoned or reasonable sex.

Margaret, Baroness Thatcher, British politician

By fifty, a man may be at the peak of his career – with power and status. A woman is washed up.

Victoria Billings, US writer

No man can call himself liberal, or radical, or even a conservative advocate of fair play, if his work depends in any way on the unpaid or underpaid labour of women at home, or in the office.

Gloria Steinem, US feminist

Men thought it natural for women to do all the boring, repetitive, or onerous chores that they themselves didn't want to do; but for women to do something interesting or intellectually stimulating was viewed as a violation of the divine order.

Barbara G. Walker, US feminist writer

He should have put his wife to work. That's the way doctors and lawyers pay for their education nowadays.

Jesamyn West (1907–84), US poet

When do you care for a man's company?

When he owns it.

How are men like noodles?

They're always in hot water, they lack taste, and they need dough.

Never marry a man for money.

You'll have to earn every penny.

A successful man is one who makes more money than his wife can spend. A successful woman is one who can find such a man.

 MEN ARE LIKE . . .

Men are like bank accounts. Without a lot of money, they don't generate much interest.

Men are like government bonds. They take so long to mature.

The husband was furious when he found out their joint bank account was empty. When he confronted his wife, she simply said, 'It's my turn.'
  'What do you mean, your turn?' yelled the husband.
  'In bed,' she explained, 'you've been making early withdrawals for years. Now it's my turn.'

This guy is walking with his friend. Suddenly he says, 'I'm a walking economy.'
  The friend replies, 'How so?'
  'My hairline is in recession, my stomach is a victim of inflation, and both of these together are putting me into a deep depression!'

A man found his credit card had been stolen. He decided not to report it, however, because the thief was spending less than his wife did.

A man goes into a tattoo shop and asks to have a £50 note tattooed on his penis. The tattoo artist asks why on earth he wants that done.

The man replies that he likes to play with his money, likes to watch his money grow and best of all, his wife can blow £50 without leaving the house.

A man rushes into his house and yells to his wife, 'Mary, pack up your things! I just won the state lottery!'

Mary replies, 'Should I pack for warm weather or cold?'

The man says, 'I don't care. Just as long as you're out of the house by noon.'

6 PIGGING IT

general slobbishness of men

The more I see of men the better I like dogs.

Madame de Staël (Anne Marie Louise Germaine, Baronne de Staël-Holstein; 1766–1817), French woman of letters

Giving a man space is like giving a dog a computer: the chances are he will not use it nicely.

Bette-Jane Raphael

Some of my best leading men have been horses and dogs.

Elizabeth Taylor, US film actress

The fantasy of every Australian man is to have two women – one cleaning and the other dusting.

Maureen Murphy

I have had my belly full of great men (forgive the expression). I quite like to read about them in the pages of Plutarch, where they don't outrage my humanity. Let us see them carved in marble or cast in bronze, and hear no more about them. In real life they are nasty creatures, persecutors, temperamental, despotic, bitter and suspicious.

George Sand (Amantine Lucie Aurore Dupin, Baronne Dudevant; 1804–76), French novelist and champion of women's rights to independence

Well, I've finally figured out that being male is the same thing, more or less, as having a personality disorder.

Carol Shields, US writer, from The Republic of Love

[Men who deride women] are commonly either conceited Fops, whose success in their Pretences to the favour of our Sex has been no greater than their Merit, and fallen very far short of their Vanity and Presumption, or a sort of morose, ill-bred, unthinking Fellows, who appear to be Men only by their Habit and Beards, and are scarce distinguishable from Brutes but by their Figure and Risibility.

Judith Drake (fl. 1696), English writer

I don't know how men are different from hogs . . . they chase after the same things: food, drink, women.

Emilia Pardo Bazán (1852–1921), Spanish novelist and stateswoman

Men are beasts and even beasts don't behave as they do.

Brigitte Bardot, French film actress

Man, as he is, is not a genuine article. He is an imitation of something, and a very bad imitation.

P. D. Ouspensky (1878–1947), Russian-born philosopher and disciple of Gurdjieff

Men are like animals – messy, insensitive and potentially violent – but they make great pets.

Anon.

Boys will be boys, and so will a lot of middle-aged men.

Kin Hubbard (Frank McKinney Hubbard; 1868–1930), US humorist

As far as I know, a single man has never vacuumed behind a couch.

Rita Rudner, US comedian

I don't want to sound sexist here, but I think men do make better [shopping-]mall Santas: men have bigger bellies, men are used to sitting for long periods of time, and men have lots of experience making promises they have no intention of keeping.

Jay Leno, US comedian and talk-show host

A good place to meet a man is at the dry cleaner's. These men usually have jobs and are hygienically responsible.

Rita Rudner, US comedian

Men fantasize about having a harem – a group of women that fulfils all their wishes. Women don't fantasize about having a male harem; that's just more men to pick up after.

Ibid.

Why we oppose votes for men . . . because men are too emotional to vote. Their conduct at baseball games and political conventions shows this, while their innate tendency to appeal to force renders them particularly unfit for the task of government.

Alice Duer Miller (1874–1942), US novelist and poet

Boys pride themselves on their drab clothing, their droopy socks, their smeared and inky skin: dirt, for them, is almost as good as wounds. They work at acting like boys. They call each other by their last names, draw attention to any extra departures from cleanliness . . . There always seem to be more of them in the room than there actually are.

Margaret Atwood, Canadian poet and novelist

All men are not slimy warthogs. Some men are silly giraffes, some woebegone puppies, some insecure frogs. But if one is not careful, those slimy warthogs can ruin it for all the others.

Cynthia Heimel, US humorist

A man's home may seem to be his castle on the outside; inside it is more often his nursery.

Clare Boothe Luce (1903–87), US writer, playwright, journalist, politician and diplomat

I've never gone anywhere where the men have come up to my infantile expectations.

Dame Rebecca West (1892–1983), British journalist, novelist and critic

Men can clean, of course, but women do clean.

Mary Lowndes (1864–1947), British feminist writer

I wanted to be alone, and what better place to choose than the sink, where neither of the men would follow me?

Barbara Pym (1913–80), British novelist

Almost nothing of any value was ever done by a man who had to take care of his own household and cookery, not to mention child care and other mundane chores of daily life.

Barbara G. Walker, US feminist writer

If housework is so fulfilling, why aren't men beating down the doors to get in on it?

Gabrielle Burton, US feminist writer

A doctor pointed out that oestrogen [the female hormone] is at its lowest level during the menstrual cycle. So at our 'worst', we are most like the way men are all the time.

Anon., from a US suburban newsletter

The scorn men express for a male who does housework is exceeded only by their aversion to a woman who doesn't.

Penney Kome, Canadian journalist

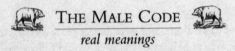

THE MALE CODE
real meanings

'Uh huh,' 'Sure, honey,' or 'Yes, dear'	*really mean . . . absolutely nothing. Their use is a conditioned response.*
I'm getting more exercise lately.	*The batteries in the remote are dead.*
Take a break, honey, you're working too hard.	*I can't hear the game over the vacuum cleaner.*
You expect too much of me.	*You want me to stay awake.*

It's a really good movie.

It's got guns, knives, fast cars, and Julia Roberts.

You know how bad my memory is.

I remember the theme tune to The Professionals, *the address of the first girl I ever kissed and the registration numbers of every car I've ever owned, but I forgot your birthday.*

I do help around the house.

I once put a dirty towel in the laundry basket.

I can't find it.

It didn't fall into my out-stretched hands, so I'm completely clueless.

What did I do this time?

What did you catch me doing?

I heard you.

I haven't the foggiest clue what you just said, and am hoping desperately that I can fake it well enough so that you don't spend the next three days yelling at me.

I missed you.	*I can't find my sock drawer, the kids are hungry and we are out of toilet paper.*
We share the housework.	*I make a mess, you clean it up.*
This relationship is getting too serious.	*You're cutting into the time I spend with my car.*

TRUE FACTS ABOUT MEN!

The woman's work that is never done is the stuff she asked her husband to do.

Go for younger men. You might as well – they never mature anyway.

Definition of a man with manners – he gets out of the bath to pee.

Scientists have just discovered something that can do the work of five men – a woman.

Men's brains are like the prison system – not enough cells per man.

There are only two four-letter words that are offensive to men – 'don't' and 'stop'.

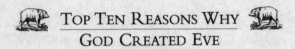

TOP TEN REASONS WHY
GOD CREATED EVE

1. God worried that Adam would always be lost in the Garden of Eden because men hate to ask for directions.

2. God knew that Adam would one day need someone to hand him the TV remote control. (Men don't want to see what's on television, they want to see WHAT ELSE is on.)

3. God knew that Adam would never buy a new fig leaf when his wore out and would therefore need Eve to get one for him.

4. God knew that Adam would never make a doctor's appointment for himself.

5. God knew that Adam would never remember which night was garbage night.

6. God knew that if the world was to be populated, men never would be able to handle childbearing.

7. As 'Keeper of the Garden', Adam would never remember where he put his tools.

8. The scripture account of the Creation indicates Adam needed someone to blame his troubles on when God caught him hiding in the Garden.

9. As the Bible says, 'It is not good for man to be alone.'

   And the number-one reason God created Eve . . .

10. When God finished the creation of Adam, He stepped back, scratched His head and said, 'I can do better than that.'

MEN ARE LIKE . . .

Men are like mascara. They usually run at the first sign of emotion.

Men are like bicycle helmets. Handy in an emergency, but otherwise they just look silly.

Men are like lava lamps. Fun to look at, but not all that bright.

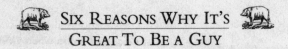

Six Reasons Why It's Great To Be a Guy

Same work, more pay.

The same hairstyle lasts for years, maybe decades.

At least a few belches are expected and tolerated.

Your belly usually hides your big hips.

One wallet and one pair of shoes, one colour, all seasons.

You can do your nails with a penknife.

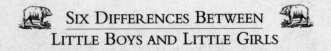

Six Differences Between Little Boys and Little Girls

You dress your little girl in her Easter Sunday best, and she'll look just as pretty when you finally make it to church an hour later.

You dress a boy in his Easter Sunday best, and he'll some-how find every muddy puddle from your home to the church, even if you drive.

A baby girl will pick up a stick and look in wonderment at what nature has made.

A baby boy will pick up a stick and turn it into a weapon.

When girls play with dolls, they like to dress them up and play house with them.

When boys play with dolls, they like to tear off the dolls' appendages.

If a girl accidentally burps, she will be embarrassed.

If a boy accidentally burps, he will follow it with a dozen forced ones.

Even at an early age, girls are attracted to boys.

At an early age, boys are attracted to dirt.

Girls turn into women.

Boys turn into bigger boys.

OTHER DIFFERENCES
BETWEEN MEN AND WOMEN

Cats

Women love cats.

Men say they love cats, but when women aren't looking, men kick cats.

Laundry

Women do laundry every couple of days.

A man will wear every article of clothing he owns, including his surgical pants that were hip about eight years ago, before he will do his laundry. When he is finally out of clothes, he will wear a dirty sweatshirt inside out, rent a van and take his mountain of clothes to the launderette – and expect to meet a beautiful woman while he is there.

Plants

A woman will ask a man to water her plants while she is on holiday. The man will water the plants. The woman returns five days later, to an apartment full of dead plants. No one knows why this happens.

What's the difference between a man and a chimpanzee?

One is hairy, smelly and always scratching its arse, and the other is a chimpanzee. Both, however, are great apes.

Why do men talk so dirty?

So they can wash their mouths out with beer.

What has eight arms and an IQ of 60?

Four men watching a football game.

Husband: 'Shall we try changing positions tonight?'
Wife: 'That's a good idea . . . you stand by the ironing board while I sit on the sofa and fart.'

Why do bald guys have holes in their pockets?

So they can run their fingers through their hair.

What do men and nappies have in common?

They are always on your arse and full of shit.

Why do men call women birds?

Because of all the worms they pick up.

Diamonds are a girl's best friends. Dogs are man's best friend. So which is the dumber sex?

What do a clitoris, an anniversary and a toilet bowl have in common?

Men always miss them.

What should you give a man who has everything?

A woman to show him how to work it.

Why can't men get mad cow disease?

Because men are pigs.

What's a man's idea of a romantic evening?

A candlelit football stadium.

How is a man like a second-hand car?

Both are easy to get, cheap and unreliable.

Why would women be better off if men treated them like cars?

At least then they would get a little attention every 6 months or 10,000 miles, whichever came first.

Why do only 10 per cent of men make it to Heaven?

Because if they all went, it would be Hell!

Why do women live longer than men?

Someone has to stick around and clean up the mess after them.

The best way to get a man to do something is to suggest he is too old for it.

The most effective way to remember your wife's birthday is to forget it once.

How is a man like the weather?
Nothing can be done to change either one of them.

Why don't men often show their true feelings?
Because they don't have any.

How do men sort their laundry?
'Filthy' and 'Filthy but Wearable'.

What would get your man to put down the toilet seat?
A sex-change operation.

What is gross stupidity?
One hundred and forty-four men in one room.

Why are men like commercials?
You can't believe a word they say.

How many honest, intelligent, caring men in the world does it take to do the dishes?

Both of them.

What do men and sperm have in common?

They both have a one-in-a-million chance of becoming human beings.

Why are jokes about blondes so short?

So men can remember them.

How many men does it take to change a roll of toilet paper?

We don't know; it has never happened.

How do you get a man to do sit-ups?

Put the remote control between his toes.

How are men and parking spots alike?

Good ones are always taken. Free ones are mostly handicapped or extremely small.

Why don't men have mid-life crises?

They're stuck in adolescence.

Why did God create a man before a woman?
You need a rough draft before you have a final copy.

How does a man take a bubble bath?
He eats beans for dinner.

Ass, n.: the masculine of 'lass'.

A man is driving up a steep, narrow mountain road. A woman is driving down the same road. As they pass each other the woman leans out the window and yells, 'PIG!'

The man immediately leans out his window and replies, 'BITCH!'

They each continue on their way, and as the man rounds the next corner, he crashes into a pig in the middle of the road.

Nature has many laws that hold fast and true. For example, a baby ape will always grow up to be an ape; likewise, a baby baboon will become an adult baboon. A baby pig will mature into a full-grown pig. A baby jackass will always become a jackass. A puppy quickly matures into a dog; a mongrel pup develops into a cur.

Yet oddly enough, women say a young man may grow up to be any one of these.

'This place is a mess! C'mon, you and I need to clean up. Your stuff is lying all over the floor, and if we don't do the laundry right now, you'll have no clothes to wear.'

What the man hears:

'Blah, blah, blah, blah, C'MON

blah, blah, blah, blah, YOU AND I

blah, blah, blah, blah, THE FLOOR

blah, blah, blah, blah, RIGHT NOW

blah, blah, blah, blah, NO CLOTHES.'

Smith goes to see his supervisor in the front office. 'Boss,' he says, 'we're doing some heavy house cleaning at home tomorrow and my wife needs me to help with the attic and the garage, moving and hauling stuff.'

'We're short-handed, Smith,' the boss replies. 'I can't give you the day off.'

'Thanks, boss,' says Smith, 'I knew I could count on you!'

A policeman was checking up about a robbery in a home. The policeman told the lady of the house, 'This is the messiest room I ever saw. You should have reported the robbery right away.'

The woman said, 'I didn't know it was a robbery. I thought my husband had been looking for a clean shirt!'

Seems God was just about done creating the universe, had a couple of left-over things in his bag of creations, so he stopped by to visit Adam and Eve in the Garden of Eden.

One of the things He had to give away was the ability to stand up and pee. 'It's a very handy thing,' God told the couple, whom He found hanging around under an apple tree. 'I was wondering if either one of you wanted that ability.'

Adam jumped up and begged, 'Oh, give that to me! I'd love to be able to do that! It seems the sort of thing a man should do. Oh please, oh please, oh please, let me have that ability. It'd be so great! When I'm working in the garden or naming the animals, I could just let it rip, I'd be so cool. Oh please, God, let it be me whom you give that gift to, let me stand and pee, oh please . . . ' On and on he went like an excited little boy.

Eve just smiled and shook her head at the display. She told God that if Adam really wanted it so badly – and it certainly seemed to be the sort of thing that would make him happy – she really wouldn't mind if Adam were the one given the ability to stand up and pee.

And so it was. And it was . . . well, good.

'Fine,' God said, looking back into the bag at the last of His left-over gifts. 'What's left here? Oh yes, multiple orgasms . . . '

CONCLUSION:
PIG OUT

Phew! If you're a man reading this little book and you've got this far, you are probably feeling more than a bit queasy by now.

If you're a woman you are probably feeling rather angry, and in agreement with this final quote from the American writer Nicole Hollander:

'What would the world be like without men?
Free of crime and full of fat, happy women.'